To
Walt + Vivian

God Bless you
for all your support for
Alaska.

Walter Hickel
3-18-95

35359
$20 "p"

D0955107

The Wit and Wisdom of Wally Hickel

The Wit and Wisdom of Wally Hickel

Compiled and edited by
Malcolm B. Roberts

SEARCHERS
PRESS
Anchorage, 1994

Published by Searchers Press
2001 Churchill Drive, Anchorage, Alaska 99517

Publisher's Cataloging in Publication Data

Roberts, Malcolm B., 1936 -
The Wit and Wisdom of Wally Hickel/compiled and edited by
Malcolm B. Roberts.
    2nd edition
    p. cm.
    Library of Congress Catalog Card Number: 94-93929

1. Hickel, Walter J. — quotations and speeches. 2. Roberts, Malcolm B.
- ideas and sayings of Walter J. Hickel. 3. Quotations - American.
4. Philosophy–Walter J. Hickel I. Title.

E838.5.H522 1994 973.928

ISBN 0-9644316-0-2: $14.95 softcover

Cover Photo by Mark Farmer
Cover design by Matt Knutson
Text design by Darrell Chambers
Printed in the United States of America

Searchers Press books are available at special discounts for
bulk purchases for sales promotions, fund raising or
educational use. Contact Searchers Press Sales Division,
807 G Street, Suite 205 B, Anchorage, Alaska 99501. Tel:
(907) 272-8644. Fax: (907) 274-8644.

*"To discover the truth, ask the very young
or the very old."*

— Napaskiak, Alaska (1978)

DISCLAIMER

The enclosed quotes are from my personal collection. The choice of which sayings to be included was mine. As they are taken out of context, they do not necessarily represent Mr. Hickel's complete views on a given subject. Perhaps some of his close admirers and family members may consider the expletives I have included to be in bad taste. But I chose each quote carefully to represent the realism of this man as I know him. And I stand by their accuracy.

—The author

DEDICATION

To Walter J. Hickel—
a man of great thoughts and great
heart.

PREFACE

Wally Hickel's love, and mine, for a new idea, powerfully expressed, produced this volume. The first edition was a gift to him on his seventieth birthday, August 18, 1989. There was only one copy published.

When he decided not to run for re-election as Alaska's governor in August 1994, I thought it was time for his friends, supporters and even his detractors to appreciate the complexity and depth of this remarkable man. The result was a mad rush during evenings and week-ends to edit a second edition, adding some of his latest ideas and phrases.

Most of these thoughts were first written on the backs of envelopes, airplane napkins, and whatever else I could lay my hands on while we traveled together in the early 1970s. I joined him during the second year he served as Secretary of the Interior in President Richard Nixon's cabinet, and then staffed his activities for three years in Alaska. Those years included months of air travel as we crisscrossed America promoting his book *Who Owns America?* They also included travels to Australia and Europe at the request of Secretary General Maurice Strong who enlisted Hickel to help advance the first United Nations Conference on the Human Environment, which was held in Stockholm, Sweden in 1972.

During these trips, we met with some of the world's great thinkers and personalities, such as anthropologist Margaret Mead, ecologist Rene Dubos, economists

Barbara Ward and Paul Samuelson, inventor Buckminister Fuller, labor giant George Meany, governor and scientist Dixie Lee Ray, think tank leader Herman Kahn, longshoreman philosopher Eric Hoffer, university president and philosopher Dr. Glenn Olds, and Hickel's great friend, industrialist and founder of the Aspen Institute, Robert O. Anderson. These meetings sparked some of the ideas captured here.

Most of the more recent quotes in this, the second edition, were jotted down during his second term as Alaska's governor, just now completed. Once again I served on his staff.

Although these bits and pieces were gathered over a period of nearly 25 years, they are mostly drawn from the seven years when I worked with him on a daily basis. Therefore they capture only a part of the range of ideas and interests which are Wally Hickel's life. As the reader will discover, the scope of his intellectual curiosity is immense.

What I especially admire is the way he relentlessly pursues the truth, whether or not it is considered conventional wisdom or politically correct. What I especially enjoy is his whimsy, his humor, his optimism.

Malcolm B. Roberts
Juneau, Alaska
December 1994

If the U.S. Congress had written the
Ten Commandments, they would be
known as the Ten Volumes.

— Walter J. Hickel

TABLE OF CONTENTS

I

The Most Precious Things on Earth

We must arrive at a moment in history when we recognize that all people are human and humans are the most precious things on earth.

What machine do you know that on a bowl of cereal in the morning, a peanut butter sandwich at lunch, and a spaghetti dinner, can do that amount of work?

The 19th century, as far as America was concerned, was the century of agriculture and westward movement. The 20th century, as far as western civilization is concerned, is the century of technology. The 21st century, as far as the world is concerned, will be the century of the human.

Have you ever met a population expert who's an optimist?

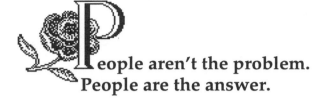

People aren't the problem.
People are the answer.

Over-crowding is the issue,
not over-population.

Think of the poverty of 100
years ago when there was only one
billion people on earth.

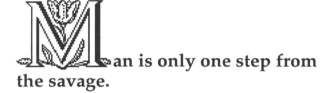**M**an is only one step from the savage.

———◆———◆———

It's taken since the beginning of time until now to realize that you can't tell what's in a man's heart by the color of his skin.

II

The Mongrel Nation

America is a mongrel nation. We are not a thoroughbred. We're not German or Irish, black or white, Christian or Jew. We are *all* those things. And we don't all get tired at once.

———◆———

There was never another nation founded as a cause. Most nations were born a nation. We created ours.

We tried to be helpful overseas in the past, and we were hurt. Because when you lead with your heart, unlike when you lead with your head, it can be much more painful. But, if America goes inward, it could drive other nations to the wall. (1975)

America's isolation is a short term thing. With communications and travel, it can't last for long. Protection is a good way to die. (1973)

I want America to fall in love again—to fall in love with her blacks and hispanics, her truly unfortunate, her truly poor, her sick and elderly—to fall in love with her slums; not to hate their ugliness, but to fall in love with the challenge to do something about them. (1973)

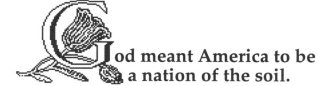

God meant America to be a nation of the soil.

Whenever we seem to lose our way, we should look back at our history, rooted in the ruts of a wagon train.

The West Coast should be the front door of America. (1962)

The early colonists were moving towards something. Not running from something.

The American idea is not the property of any one country.

America is the only conscience the world has. If others falter, we come to their aid. But , make no mistake, if America falters, no other nation will be able to save us.

Yes, we made a mistake in Vietnam. But we didn't at Normandy, or Gettysburg, or Valley Forge.

III

Ownership

In reality, one has but a lease on ownership during one's lifetime. The success or failure of how something is used depends on how it is left.

There are some things we will always own in common. No one will ever homestead the ocean.

If no one owns something, no one cares.

No matter how great, how vast or how simple individual ownership might be, it must be looked upon as a passing thing. What good would it be if one owned it all and left an emptiness in passing?

What we must now realize for the first time in America is that it is really a collective world, but one in which we live so privately. Without concern for the other person, for his desires and wants, activities for strictly private gain become destructive not only to others but eventually to oneself.

As we look at the globe, seven-eighths of which is covered with water, we can see that it is truly a collective world. No one country owns the air or the water that runs from the world's rivers into a common sea. No one nation can lay claim to the moon, the planets, and the stars. So we must work together.

IV

The Inexhaustible Earth

We'll never run out of resources. The only thing
we might run out of is imagination.

I might be worried if this
were the only planet we could
see, the only star in the sky.

The question of world
hunger in not a lack of food but lack
of distribution.

The resources of this earth are inexhaustible. Because God made man's mind inexhaustible.

The great frontier of tomorrow will be to discover the world's emptiness.

We haven't even scratched the surface of the earth. All we've done is slide around on the skin of the apple. We haven't even thought about the core.

V

Alaska

Alaska is a country of backpackers in the summertime, skiers in the winter, hunters in the fall, and people with anticipation in the spring.

Alaska, this unique piece of geology, is a bridge between the anglo-western, Judeo-Christian, European world and that part of the world that is not necessarily anglo, western or Judeo-Christian.

Alaska's political ties are with America, but our economic ties are with the Pacific.

Alaska is an Owner State. That's real. You can't wish it away.

◆————————————◆

Alaska enjoys a democratic, free enterprise, incentive system just like the rest of the nation. But here the government owns virtually all of the resources. And that's the difference.

◆————————————◆

In an Owner State, government cannot just regulate. It must initiate, innovate and advocate.

The job of the governor of an Owner State is to be the foreman of the ranch.

———◆———

Alaska has a special magic that lures people north. It has a spirit that is almost spiritual. (1992)

———◆———

There is no vision, no hope, no future, no agenda for Alaska, if your only ideology, if your only philosophy, if your only cause is to cut the budget. (Juneau 1994)

Alaska must be a place where the human spirit can grow because we respect every person, regardless of age, race or heritage. In short — one country, one people. (1991)

———◆———

I don't just talk about subsistence hunting and fishing. I believe in it. The people on the river system should have first call on the fish. But Alaska's future depends on creating a system that is fair to all.

———◆———

Alaska's North Slope is the most environmentally sensitive oil field on the globe — bar none.

The secret to the North is an iron wheel and a rail.

Ultimately, we should extend the Alaska Railroad across the high country to the Seward Peninsula. Not just to do it, but to open the country for people to see. The railroad is not an old fashioned idea. It is the finest environmental transportation system in the Arctic.

Cold countries have to have a reason. Warm countries don't. They'll survive walking on the beaches.

Everyone has his dream of fantasy about Alaska. He lives in his fenced little yard in a warm climate. He mixes up these dreams of fantasy with reality. He has no desire to live here; and most will never come here to see.

If Russia hadn't sold Alaska to America, we would be free now, too.

(Talking about their new freedom with a group of Russian military officers dining at the Governor's mansion in Juneau—1992)

America has fouled its rivers and lakes and encouraged its great cities to jam themselves with millions of people. The rest of the country has committed the crime. But Congress wants Alaska to pay the penalty. (1992)

Our task is not to follow America, but to educate America. (1993)

Eventually, we will see the opening of the Arctic National Wildlife Refuge despite some South 48 congressmen who believe Alaska needs more wilderness. I'm looking forward to when they clean up their own states—starting with that embarassing, junk-filled rail corridor from New York to Washington, DC.

(State of the Budget—1993)

Our Statehood lawsuits are setting a precedent for the world. If the U.S. doesn't honor its contract with Alaska, it's a threat to our treaties with all other nations.

◆————————————◆

Alaska will never have enough political power in Washington, DC. To win, we have to adjudicate.

We've got to take it back first.

(In answer to a news media question regarding the threat by Russian nationalist Vladimir Zhirinovsky to take Alaska back—1994)

◆————————————◆

The EPA's land fill regulations don't fit Alaska. In a landfill in the Arctic, all you have is frozen crap.

There would be no Permanent Fund without Prudhoe Bay. But with a Permanent Fund mentality, you would have had no Prudhoe Bay.

The Permanent Fund won't give you a permanent economy.

Alaskans have been thinking like the grandchildren of the pioneer who made a fortune. They criticize and joke about "old grandad," but they live off his money. And when that money starts to run out, they are afraid and don't know how to act. (1992)

Alaska has been to Disneyland since Prudhoe Bay. It's time to get back to work. (1991)

I still get criticized for the ice road we punched through that first year to get to the North Slope. And yet that road helped change Alaska. It wasn't just a road to somewhere. It opened up the minds, the hearts and the hopes of Alaskans. (1992)

Why ship out our oil when it sells for only $11 a barrel? We should shut down the pipeline. Let's not give our oil away. Why should we give away our inheritance, while the oil companies make money?

Alaska must be given a chance to grow. No young person can build self-esteem if all he hears is, "You can't. You can't. You can't." I say, "You can! We will!" (1991)

America wants everyone born an adult. Well everywhere else had its infancy, its adolescence.

In Alaska we've made mistakes. But they were mistakes of doing, not of intent.

If God had to put resources
on earth for man to use, we should be
grateful he put them on the North
Slope of Alaska; not in the Wrangell
Mountains or Yosemite National Park.

◆————————————◆

No one is ever going to buy a
lot and retire at Prudhoe Bay.

During the early days in Alaska, it wasn't them and us. It was *all* of us.

———◆———

Sure we can disagree among ourselves, but when we walk out of the country, it should be Alaska First.

VI

It's Time to Think Rich Again

Address to the
Chamber of Commerce, Sitka, Alaska
January 18, 1986

Before coming here today, I thought about Alaska and all my years here, and what they mean to me. I found my answer on an old wooden plaque that's been in my office for years. Dag Hammerskjold's words are written upon it, and to me these words describe the perfect motto for an Alaskan.

"For all that has been . . . thanks. For all that will be . . . yes."

We have turned into a state of money changers.

"For all that has been . . . thanks." Words that understand the battles, the wins and losses; words that express how grateful I am for the opportunity to be a part of these battles and to be a part of the pioneering spirit that shaped a new state.

"For all that will be . . . yes." Words that recognize the obligation we all have to the future of Alaska; a future that will contain new wins and new losses. But it is a future of such hope . . . and promise . . . and excitement . . . that the challenge is accepted with a full heart.

We used to say "North to the future" in this state . . . and believed every word of it. We were always trying to prove our potential. We thought big ideas, and we were willing to put in the grunt work to make these ideas happen.

Today, I sense a different mood. Since Prudhoe Bay, which was the most exciting opportunity this state ever had to say "yes" to the future, we have turned into a state of money changers.

We used to say, "Let's go."
Now we say, "Give me."

We used to say, "North to the future." Now we ask, "Do we have a future?"

You cannot save yourself rich.

We've been so busy counting our money, we've lost our guts.

I've been in Alaska for 45 years. In all these years I've learned one basic lesson. It's a lesson they don't teach in school. It's a lesson of the streets. A survival lesson. There is no wealth without production. You cannot save yourself rich. You can only produce yourself rich.

Alaska, in the 45 years I've been here, has learned that lesson and forgotten it. As a result, Alaska has gone from being a rich state without money, to a poor state with a large cash surplus. We're not poor; we're thinking poor. It's time to think rich again, and bring back the environment of hope.

Daniel Boorstin, one of the foremost historians of our time, writes about the people who made America great. He calls them go-getters. In my book, *Who Owns America?*, I call them searchers. These are the people who went in search of what others had never imagined was there to find; the people who made something out of nothing. The people who said "yes" to the future.

When I arrived here in 1940, the federal railroad was the economy of Anchorage. In the rest of the Territory, there was a little mining, a little timber, and a lot of fish traps, owned by outsiders.

The onset of World War II forced America to discover Alaska. The military arrived, and some of them defected and became Alaskans.

After World War II, a lot of people talked of the "end of the world." But the optimists carried us through those hard times. In 1957, oil was discovered on the Kenai, and we were on our way again.

Then we gained statehood. Dear God . . . and I say that as a prayer of thanks . . . Dear God, those were exciting days!

We did more than sew a star on the flag. We sewed on a brand new kind of star . . . one that represented a brand new kind of state. America's first, America's only owner state.

Wealth means production, and land is the means of production. For us to make it as a state, we had to have land. We probably could have been a state as early as 1952, but the 23 million acres they offered us was not enough. We had to risk asking for more. That was our battle.

We received 100 million acres, but the argument over our full rights rages on. Today, when I hear people ask, "What's happening to 40 million acres of Native corporation land?" I want to ask, "What are we doing with the 100 million acres of our own land?" That 100 million acres makes us, all Alaskans, the largest "Native" corporation.

> **Wealth means production, and land is the means of production.**

Before Prudhoe Bay, Alaska was constantly capital short. We relied on the federal government, and sometimes outside industry, to keep us in clean socks.

I remember as a young man, as Governor and as Secretary of the Interior, pushing to have the Arctic developed. Fighting both here and in Washington, DC, we overcame many obstacles, and eventually Prudhoe Bay began to produce.

Money is not secure wealth. It is merely a medium of exchange.

For more than ten years now, virtually all of Alaska's economy has come from one oilfield. How many other economies, cities, states, or countries can you name that are based on one project?

Money is not secure wealth. It is merely a medium of exchange to acquire assets that produce. Alaska's citizens have become like the children of *Dynasty* on television, shoring up an inheritance instead of creating a new future for themselves.

We have a Permanent Fund all right, but not a permanent economy. While the Permanent Fund is a good idea, just having a savings account is not enough.

Let's ask ourselves, "What are we doing now to get things started?"

As former Treasury Secretary William Simon said, "We need a long term strategy with benchmarks: What's our target in 50 years, 20 years, 10 years?"

Alaska will still have more money from Prudhoe Bay over the next 20 years than we ever dreamed of in 1959.

With care, imagination, and determination, let's take a look at all the resources we own. We are hindered only by the limits of our own minds.

Alaska must reassert itself as the rightful owner of the land and assume the obligation of ownership, an obligation to the total, to think in the interest of the total, to develop some areas, while conserving others.

A while back I was talking to author James Michener. He said, "People generate their own economy . . . people come before the cities . . . every civilization in history has been encouraged to expand . . . except Alaska."

Why should Alaska be different? Let's move forward and create our own opportunities. Let's get our natural gas to market . . . our natural market on the Pacific Rim.

Let's clean up our roads, rebuild our cities . . . instead of waiting for a war or natural disaster . . . expand our railroads, and bring our parks up to standard.

We have the technology to reap the riches of our land without raping it.

We own our fisheries. Let's behave like we own them. Let's help Alaska's fishermen rival the Japanese and Russians. There is talk of kicking out the foreign fishermen. Before we do it, we should ask ourselves a serious question: Are we going to kick out our markets with them?

We own our land. Let's behave like we own it. For the past few years Alaska has been described as the "last great battleground between the developers and the conservationists." Baloney. This is an artificial battleground. We have the technology to reap the riches of the land without raping it.

Let's be the most exciting and innovative place in the world.

Let's be the most exciting and innovative place in the world. To be a land of opportunity, the state government must shed its bureaucratic personality and act like an owner. The government has to be an advocate, not an adversary.

Our governor has to be someone who will govern, not just be the governor. In essence, he is the foreman of the ranch. The one who makes the tough decisions. His job is to make things happen.

And if Alaska refuses to move forward, we are likely to become another lesson of failure, something to read about in a dusty history book. History has shown us that when a country stops believing in economic growth, its citizens go hungry. Alaska will be no different. This is not hunger in terms of food. It's hunger in the sense of loss of vitality, a steady decline as people lose jobs, as small businesses close, and as more houses are left vacant.

Alaska became great by having people who wouldn't surrender, who didn't give up, because they saw beyond the here and now, into the promise of tomorrow.

To look over the horizon and see our potential makes it disheartening to live below average. We need people who know about Alaska and care about it, people who aren't satisfied with being average.

Alaskans must rediscover the spirit that existed before Prudhoe Bay, when we thought we were rich beyond our wildest dreams . . . and that richness was of the spirit.

Looking back and looking forward, I hope that Alaska will always be a land of opportunity for everyone. I hope that as a state, we can always say: "For all that has been . . . Thanks. For all that will be . . . Yes."

VII

The Color of the
Environment

Our job is to care about the *total* environment: people, people's needs and nature.

— The Earth Summit,
   Rio de Janeiro 1992

It is relatively easy to be a champion for the walrus or the beaver or the caribou or a favorite lake, but somebody somewhere has to be responsible for the total.

We shall look back on the smog of today with the same disbelief as when we look back on the plagues of the Middle Ages. (1973)

By replacing the gas tank in your car with a propane-like bottle, we can solve the majority of the world's man-made air pollution.

People wonder how much it will cost to protect our environment. Who is going to pay the bills? The truth is we all are. The cost is to care. If we care enough, it will be done right.

Every person, every year of his life, should be asked to plant a tree and watch it grow. This would not only create a great culture, it would create a great people.

A tree can teach you a lot. From seed to maturity is just about a man's lifetime. There's no way you can speed up a tree.

The color of the environment is not just green. It's real.

◆————————————◆

If a man is cold and hungry and unemployed, he is in an ugly environment, regardless of the beauty of his surroundings.

◆————————————◆

In a relatively short time, we have seen the environment move from a cause to a crusade to a special interest. (1971)

The people in the environmental movement are protesting their parents.

———————◆———————

Governor Jerry Brown of California says the OCS* is delicate. I agree with him. And so is the oil shale in Colorado, the coal fields of Montana, the hydro projects, nuclear, Georges Banks off the East Coast, the North Slope . . . they are all delicate. But who is going to care for man's needs? (1975)

*The Outer Continental Shelf

The doers have done more
for the environment than the don'ters.

You can only clean up
the environment
with progress.

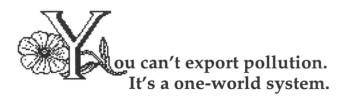

You can't export pollution.
It's a one-world system.

If there's a standoff between environmentalists and developers, the one who will win is the one who meets the needs of people.

Ultimately the individual has to pay for a clean environment. The consumer pays for everything. It goes back to what we want to pay for.

If man asphalts the globe and destroys himself, nature will eventually return. Man is only hurting himself.

The challenge is not to isolate man from nature, but to make man compatible with nature.

———————◆———————

A true environmentalist is a caveman without a match.

———————◆———————

Walk the country in your mind. It's the greatest trip on earth.

If the needs of man aren't met, the environmental needs of nature will never be met.

If you're selfish, nothing happens.

(On why he didn't mind when the City of Anchorage wanted to put the Coastal Trail through his property on Fish Creek.)

People sometimes imagine that "quality of life" is something down the road, something to wait for. It's not. The quality of life is now.

The quality of life can be seen in clean streets, in the flowers along the roads and in people's front yards. It can be seen in the architecture of our buildings. It can be seen in the opportunity for our young people to find jobs. It can be seen in feeling safe on our streets and in our homes. It can be seen, most of all, in the spirit of the people. (1994)

VIII

Michelangelo, where are you?

Cultures aren't created by nature. Cultures are created by man. Someone has to make them happen. That means someone has to care.

❖————————————————❖

No government could have created San Francisco. It would have been so dull, so stereotyped. The greatness is in the difference created by different people.

❖————————————————❖

In America, it's the builders who will create our culture.

If God hadn't wanted growth, he wouldn't have made sex so inviting.

It's ironic how we honor the builders of the past, the brilliant mathematicians who designed the pyramids, the artists of Greece who fashioned their philosophy in stone, the men of God in Europe who constructed cathedrals to elevate the human spirit. These are the champions of civilizations past. And yet, the builders of today are viewed as the bad guys.

They used to roll out the red carpet for the doers. Now they roll out the criticism, the restrictions, the bad press. Developer has become a dirty word.

There is nothing permanent enough in this country to fit a Michelangelo. So how can there be a Michelangelo? How can he come forward? He cannot do a mural in a steel and glass courthouse that after a few years has a sign on it that reads, "Demolish. I-95 passing through."

We fly to Europe to see the things we tear down here in America. The old world understood it and the new world missed it — that all motivation is not economic. Our society is so economic that nothing is lasting. The old Europeans did it for love.

We now have a society of glittering junk.

When building a building, architecture doesn't cost you money. It makes you money.

Civilizations are what they think they are.

America will establish a culture through its retired people, because they will respect the old.

When the no-growth group fights the all-out developer the result is ugliness. When you work together, you create a culture.

IX

The Price of Freedom

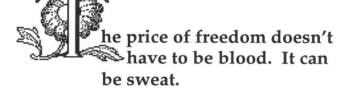

The price of freedom doesn't have to be blood. It can be sweat.

No other society on earth demands as much of the individual citizen as a free society.

If we keep looking for the lowest common denominator in democracy, we'll become the lowest common denominator.

There's no freedom in welfare. You're enslaved to the system.

———◆———

Freedom includes being confident enough to walk out of whatever situation you are in and earn a living as a carpenter.

———◆———

You are free to swing your fist at the end of your arm until it lands on someone's nose.

In democracy, the critic isn't responsible. He has a license to destroy.

An individual can have so much freedom that society can't get anything done.

Some of the media want to control government without the responsibility of governing.

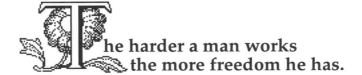The harder a man works the more freedom he has.

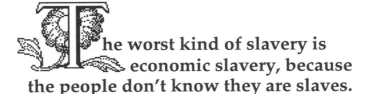The worst kind of slavery is economic slavery, because the people don't know they are slaves.

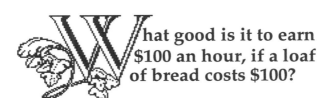What good is it to earn $100 an hour, if a loaf of bread costs $100?

X

Energy — the Great Emancipator

There's an unusual tie-in between energy and poverty, energy and peace, energy and life.

◆——————————◆

Show me any place on earth where there is a shortage of energy, and I'll show you basic poverty.

◆——————————◆

The answer in the developing nations begins with energy. Freedom depends on energy. So does hope.

There's no shortcut to anything. It all takes energy—any human activity.

———◆———

Cheap electricity is not about turning on a light. It's about turning on opportunity.

The most highly concentrated form of vegetable oil is called crude.

❖————————————❖

Those who say oil is evil don't understand energy. And those who don't understand energy, don't understand the environment.

❖————————————❖

If we wait until we are faced by a dramatic oil shortage, the cries of those of us who care about the environment will be unheard above the roar of heavy machinery.

Think of the tremendous energy in a thunderstorm or in an erupting volcano.

Look at energy as the way to eliminate pollution.

If you would put the scientific minds of the world together you'd have fusion. Then there would be unlimited energy. They'll be able to run a plant to power San Francisco out of someone's basement.

When we finally discover a sun in a test tube, we will hold it in our hands and say, "How obvious. It was there all the time."

A civilization without energy is a civilization in slavery.

They had great engineers 2000 years before Christ. They figured out time down to the second. They built the world's greatest monuments. But the only thing they had for energy was humans.

ertain people want to drive a Cadillac but not produce energy. They want to export pollution. In reality, they are saying, "Let other people's children choke on smog and play in polluted streams. Let other nations' wildlife be destroyed. But we must protect our own."
(Geneva, Switzerland—1973)

od showed us how to store energy in a tree. When we burn the tree, the suns comes out.

verything stores up energy from the sun. Why does a moose eat the leaves and branches of a tree? The leaves have stored up a little bit of energy. The limbs a little more.

rass stores it. It burns a little while. Coal stores it up more. It burns a little longer. The highest concentration of sunlight we know is in crude oil.

he speed of light is not the ultimate. It's the speed of thought.

XI

Renters of Money

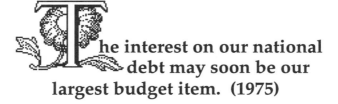

he interest on our national debt may soon be our largest budget item. (1975)

⬥————————————⬥

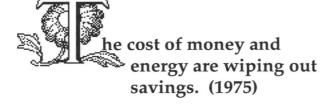

he cost of money and energy are wiping out savings. (1975)

⬥————————————⬥

e are becoming a nation of renters of money. (1967)

Money doesn't belong to
the banks. It's the people's money.

◆————————◆

Banks should be like super-
markets. Money is a commodity.

XII

Real Wealth

There is no wealth without pro-duction. Someone has to dig a hole, cut a tree, catch a fish.

◆━━━━━━━━━◆

Without production all you have is a man standing naked. His only fire is from a flintrock. His only habitation a cave. Without production, where does he get his axe, his glass, his stove, his chimney?

◆━━━━━━━━━◆

The manipulation of money does not increase the wealth of a nation.

Wealth is education, roads and schools.

If no one is out there digging in the ground, what are you going to stand in line for?

No war was ever fought over money. We have mixed up money with wealth.

There is nothing free. Even if I give you a house, someone had to cut the tree, mill the board, make the wire.

You don't need money to make money. You need resources. You need knowledge. And hard work.

Gold doesn't have to be the foundation to economics. FDR announced Germany was bankrupt because it had no gold. But Hitler switched to the barter system.

You can be as rich as God. But if you have no hope, you are as poor as dirt.

XIII

Peace and War

I do not have such a low opinion of the American people as to think that they can only be motivated by war.

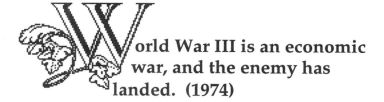

World War III is an economic war, and the enemy has landed. (1974)

We've got to build a fair society if we want world peace.

Some people say it'll take a war for America to find itself. I say it takes a leader. Someone who can spank the do-gooders, the corporations, the unions. Someone who can create the desire to work.

War and peace is the emotional issue, but not the real issue. There is always something deeper.

Wars are no longer winnable. (1972)

XIV

Liberals and Conservatives

Government must care for the helpless. Government must not make people helpless by the care it provides.

Some conservatives have made out government to be the enemy. But we cannot have America without government. We might have too much government. But we need more good, honest government.

The liberals, unable to bring the poor up, want to cut the rich down. If you tear everyone down to where everyone lives in a hovel, then there will be no one to raise you up.

The conservative today wants to forget about the things he doesn't want to believe, the realism of the poor, a smoggy sky, the unemployed. (1975)

❖————————————❖

The liberals don't have the guts to face up to freedom because they hate success. Instead of putting guidelines on success, they destroy it.

❖————————————❖

The conservatives hate government because they think it's in their way. They don't realize that for society to work government cannot be the enemy. Government must be the friend.

Government the world over is not efficient. It's just necessary.

———◆———

Christ wasn't a liberal. He was real.

———◆———

The Far Right is good at criticism. But the Far Right can't govern.

In politics it's only when you play games that you get in trouble. It's only if you want it too bad that you don't stay free.

XV

Leadership

We need men and women in government who are not looking for a job, but who want to do a job.

In the governor's office, everyone should have an audience. But no one should have a claim. (1967)

Don't worry about government when it's being criticized. Worry about it when no one gives a damn.

 emocracy wasn't designed to build great civilizations.

 here's no way a public hearing can design a road.

 e need leaders not managers.

It's not a case of knowing what to do but having the guts to do it.

◆————————————◆

Machiavelianism worked when communications were slow. But today everyone knows if you are a phony.

◆————————————◆

It's an illusion that Congress can straighten out America. It's the role of Congress to legislate. It's the role of the executive to lead.

You cannot govern with legislation. There's no flexibility.

If the people see action, they see hope.

Words are like drugs. Action is the cure. Americans have been fed drugs so long they're immune.

The fear of the decision has caused tremendous wrongs in the world. When I was Secretary, lack of fear made the Interior Department come alive. We weren't so brilliant, but we didn't fear the decision.

◆————————◆

Not that the world agreed with everything I did, but they trusted me. They may agree with President Nixon, but they don't trust him. (1972)

◆————————◆

Every executive in government should first have two or three years in contracting. The contractor has to race against the clock to put himself out of business.

When you're faced with evil you have to be brutal. That's when brutality is so acceptable.

◆━━━━━━━━━◆

A leader must do a thing when it's right; not when it's opportune.

◆━━━━━━━━━◆

Washington, DC believes that everyone has a price. Washington, DC didn't understand Wally Hickel. (1971)

XVI

The Arctic

As the world population grows, the lands within the temperate and tropical climates will be used more and more for living and enjoyment. For the resources we need, mankind will look to the Arctic, the oceans and outer space.

Man will not change the Arctic as much as the Arctic will change man.

The Arctic is probably the most misunderstood place on earth. It is even more mysterious than the moon.

The primary element that must be conquered in the Arctic is not the cold. It's the fear.

In the Arctic, we know the difference between those who come up to make a living and those who come up to make a killing.

XVII

Sustainable Living in the North

Address to the
Fifth World Wilderness Congress
Tromsø, Norway
September 25, 1993

I salute the World Wilderness Congress for dedicating a portion of your agenda to "Sustainable Living in the Arctic." From my perspective, and the perspective of most Alaskans, the advocates of wilderness preservation sometimes forget the human element.

To many in the temperate climates, "down there, looking up," the high latitudes are seen as cold, remote and as mysterious as the moon. But those of us who live here look at the Arctic differently. We don't look up. We don't look down. We look around.

To us, the Arctic is home. The Arctic is heritage. The Arctic is our here and now, and our hereafter.

Today, I have come to Tromsø both to attend this conference and The Northern Forum Conference, which I will chair. The Northern Forum is a young organization of 14 Arctic regions which addresses the unique challenges of the Arctic on a region-to-region basis.

I speak today for those who have lived in the North for generations and for those who, like myself, have enjoyed an adult life here, in my case, for 53 years.

To understand sustainable living in the Arctic, you have to have sustained thinking in the Arctic. You have to live it, over time.

We don't look down. We don't look up. We look around.

Alaska has more acreage in legally-designated Wilderness than the other 49 united states combined. When those reserves are added to other restricted lands in which mineral entry is forbidden, or so complex it is uneconomic, they total 171 million acres.

To understand sustainable living in the Arctic, you have to have sustained thinking in the Arctic. You have to live it, over time.

That is the size of the state of Texas or, in European terms, just over twice the size of this wonderful nation of Norway.

But sustainable living requires more than preservation. It requires stewardship.

After reassuming the governorship of Alaska in 1990, I set out to put the tragic 1989 Exxon Valdez oil spill behind us. I negotiated a global legal settlement with Exxon Corporation for 1 billion dollars. Since then, we have turned Prince William Sound into a living laboratory. And we have dedicated some of the settlement fund to enhance the affected areas and to purchase important habitat; such as 22,000 acres of private in-holdings in wonderful Kachemak Bay State Park.

I can say with some pride, Prince William Sound is once again the world's most beautiful natural recreation area. It's hard to imagine the incredible combination of fjords, Alps-like mountains and over 100 glaciers, some so high up they appear to be rivers of ice hanging in the sky.

In Alaska, we are as proud of our development accomplishments as we are of our environmental victories. And sustainable living requires both.

The Arctic will never compete with the rest of the world for people. But the Arctic is rich in the resources people need.

The Arctic will never compete with the rest of the world for people. But the Arctic is rich with the resources the people need. Alaska produces 25 percent of our nation's oil, and many other products.

At our North Slope, nature condensed a continent of food into an ocean of oil. Our oil development is the finest anywhere in the Arctic world; some say in the entire world.

With state oversight, industry has shrunk the size of the drilling "footprint" to one quarter of what was necessary when we began 20 years ago. Drill cuttings and muds are now re-injected deep into the earth. No waste products are left on the surface. I urge you all to visit and to examine these pioneering marvels.

Now, to discuss my theme, let's examine *"Ten Lessons Learned from Sustainable Living in the Arctic."*

Lesson #1.   *It is a collective world.*

As the indigenous peoples learned long ago, in a cold, harsh environment, you have to care about others. You waste nothing. You share to survive. You care for the total. Every hunter's prize is a gift, not just to that hunter, but to his family and village.

Throughout the world, this same sense of shared responsibility must now be awakened as we become sensitive to the needs of the environment. Pollution knows no borders. All rivers eventually run into a common sea. All living things breathe the common air.

Yes, it is a collective world, but one in which we live so privately. Without concern for other people, for their needs and wants, activities for strictly private gain become destructive, not only to others but eventually to oneself.

esson #2. *Change is a natural law. Welcome it.*

In the Far North, we observe that nothing changes the environment as much as nature. We see it in our volcanoes, our earthquakes, and our rivers, most of which don't run blue; they run rich with the colors of a changing earth.

In the North, we do not fear change. We understand that when civilizations are not allowed to grow, the harvest is revolution.

esson #3. *Government cannot be the enemy. Government must be the friend.*

In some societies, it has become the fashion to attack and ridicule government. But in the Arctic, where there is very little private land, government cannot be the enemy. Government must be the friend.

This is certainly true of Alaska. Government must regulate to make sure that economic interests don't exploit the land and the people. But it must also advocate. Unless someone in government says "yes," there will be no sustainable economy.

esson #4.   *People are the most precious things on earth.*

At the United Nations conference on the human environment in Stockholm, Sweden in 1972, the chairman of the Chinese delegation, Tang ke, challenged those who would stop development.

"We cannot stop eating for fear of choking," he scoffed.

But the phrase he said that will last forever was this: "People are the most precious things on earth." Any parent knows what he was saying. And people in the Arctic need help. As cultures meet and clash, we find confusion and despair. Alcoholism and suicides are rampant.   What do we do? Our discovery is this. By taking away people's work, whether hunting, trapping or fishing, in exchange for a government check, we steal their self-worth.

The best social program is a job. Work means more than a paycheck. It provides a sense of meaning. Without that fundamental, life isn't worth living.

esson #5.   *There is no wealth without production.*

Sustainable living in the Arctic does not mean making computer chips. Our challenge, our opportunity, is to address "sustainable living in a resource economy."

People have to use resources. That is a fact of life. To live on earth, someone has to harvest God's gifts — cut a tree, catch a fish, dig a hole. If no one is digging in the ground, or harvesting the sea, what are you going to stand in line for?

Most people who live in the temperate, tropic and sub-tropic climates will eventually insist that development activities take place somewhere else — "not in my back-yard."

Therefore, the resources of the future will come from the Arctic, the Antarctic, the oceans and space. In the case of the Arctic, instead of fearing to use resources, together, let's use them wisely.

Most nations would agree that fifty percent of their land would be a reasonable percentage for creating an economic foundation. But in my lifetime and in the lifetime of my children, we will not develop even one percent of Alaska. I believe that will also be true throughout most of the Arctic.

To begin with, we must inventory our lands *before* they are set aside for a single purpose. Let's invent a new yard-stick that measures the full range of values important to our people — economics, space for our communities, the need to subsist off the land, and the intangibles such as the value of a wilderness or a sunset.

When it comes to economic values, we must start with our energy resources. Show me any area on earth where there is a shortage of energy, and I'll show you basic poverty.

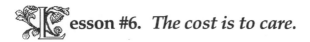# esson #6. *The cost is to care.*

Cleaning up pollution is no longer a luxury. It is an imperative. The best time to pay for the cost of making a product pollution-free is when we make the product.

Some people ask, "But how much will that cost?" The cost is to care. If you truly care, reasonable standards can be met, as long as they are based on science and are subscribed to by all competitors.

And this is important. There must be a level playing field. In Alaska, we strongly oppose those who, based on ignorance of the Arctic, demand standards of us not accepted elsewhere. This mentality, based on an anti-development bias, prevents us from exploring for oil in a small set-aside in the 19 million acre Arctic National Wildlife Refuge, east of Prudhoe Bay. This isn't reasonable.

It is an insidious form of colonialism under a new name.

esson #7. *When no one owns something, no one cares.*

No one owns the oceans. No one will ever buy a lot in the ocean or homestead there. This lack of ownership has turned the great fishing ground of the North Pacific into a battleground, a mad scramble to catch our valuable marine species.

When challenged, a fisherman replies, "If I don't catch the last fish, someone else will."

The whale was the first victim. Then, in our part of the Arctic, it was the king crab. Scientists wondered what caused the sudden collapse of the king crab population. Some thought it might be a disease. Yes! It was a disease called *greed.*

The lesson is to harvest living resources on the basis of sustained yield. This requires oversight and multi-national cooperation.

As Secretary of the Interior in 1970, in the face of angry opposition, I placed all eight species of great whales on the U.S. endangered species list.

At the 1972 Stockholm conference, I was instrumental in lobbying for a resolution for a ten-year moratorium on whaling.

Now, scientists of the International Whaling Commission estimate there are eighty thousand minke whales in the North Atlantic. Harvesting a few hundred a year will not harm the stocks and will continue a time-honored Norwegian way of life, not dissimilar to our Eskimo whaling tradition in Alaska.

 **esson #8.**   *We must care for the total environment — people, people's needs and nature.*

Sometimes in our drive for economic progress or our commitment to protect nature, we forget about people and their needs.

In eastern Russia, Northern Canada, and Alaska, the carving of soapstone and ivory is a tradition that fits a subsistence lifestyle. Recently, in order to stop poachers who have been killing walruses illegally, well-meaning U.S. law placed a ban on international ivory sales. We are already seeing the harm this is doing to our Eskimo people, both financial and psychological.

Instead, we should use modern technology to identify ivory that has been legally obtained. Or else we may end up preserving the species and destroying people who have lived in harmony with nature for thousands of years.

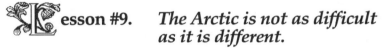 esson #9.   *The Arctic is not as difficult as it is different.*

The greatest challenge for those of us who live in the Arctic is to cope with decisions made in the South that don't work in the North. Mostly, these policies are not born of malice, but of ignorance.

For instance, when building in the Arctic, heat is your enemy, cold is your friend.

At the North Slope, oil drilling mostly takes place during the winter. Heavy rigs move across the frozen, ice-covered tundra without leaving a trace. They operate from a frozen drilling pad.

But we don't have all the answers. Our greatest environmental problems in the Arctic are solid waste disposal, fuel storage, and high cost energy.

It's a different world, and it requires different answers.

Our new-found cooperation among the regions of The Northern Forum will help us find these answers and share them with each other. That is our best hope.

esson #10. *The greatest frontier is within ourselves.*

Alaska has been known as the "last frontier." But the truth is, there will be frontiers as long as there are humans.

Every child born is given new frontiers to explore. God's way to test us is to give us our own frontiers. The frontiers are in the heart and in the mind.

The days of pioneering have just begun. The frontier of this generation is to preserve our values of old and to welcome the new. We can work together to improve our economies, elevate our people who are in poverty, and create a culture we are proud of.

We invite you of the World Wilderness Congress to join us in this task. Who knows? We may become a model for the world.

XVIII

Attitude

Man survives on fear but he lives on hope.

Victory or defeat is all in the mind. It has nothing to do with the score.

Failure is only failure if you dwell on it.

You win or lose in the mind. That's why I am a little bit of a loner. People think I am aloof.

———◆———◆———

People fear an economic depression. I fear more a depression of the spirit.

———◆———◆———

A searcher is a combination of the dreamer and the doer, the contented man and the ambitious man, all molded into one. He is a man who no matter what he accomplishes isn't satisfied.

From a speech in Fairbanks, describing the kind of people Alaska needs—1955

I love the patience of a stormy sea, the silence of its anger.

The power of the people can achieve what billions of federal dollars cannot begin to do.

Every human has competitiveness in him. Even in the most remote corner of Africa. Show him a light, and he'll go towards it.

Patience can be a cop-out for someone who doesn't want to do anything.

If you know something is going to happen, even if you don't like it, you'd better face it.

If you know you *have* to do something, make it fun. Race yourself against it, even if it's just shoveling a pile of dirt.

Enthusiasm will make mistakes.
But enthusiasm will clean up
those mistakes.

◆━━━━━━━━━◆

There is nothing built on this earth
that couldn't be built better the
second time around.

◆━━━━━━━━━◆

On October 1, be optimistic.
The days start getting longer
the month after next.

◆━━━━━━━━━◆

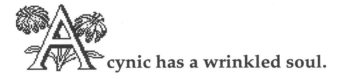

A cynic has a wrinkled soul.

When you put pessimism and optimism together any time in history, optimism always wins.

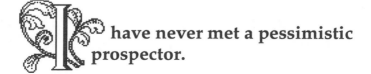

One man who cares is worth a million just talking to each other about the problem.

I have never met a pessimistic prospector.

All pioneers are optimists. The pessimist never gets out of town.

Bad thoughts destroy the person who thinks them.

If the world record for the mile was six minutes today, there would be no way you could run it in four minutes.

Trust your friends and cultivate your enemies.

I trust a man until proved otherwise. In my business, I have never checked a cash register or a bank account.

———◆———

Trust has hurt me more than anything on earth, but I wouldn't be anywhere without it. They call it being naive. Bullshit! Those who play it safe never get up to bat.

———◆———

If you can carry the trust of a small child as late in life as possible then you will stay young longer.

There are no "limits to growth" of the human mind and spirit.

◆————————————————◆

It doesn't matter if he's a pro, no one in the world is better than you are, if you are concerned.

◆————————————————◆

I like to give it everything I have. And then walk away.

Miracles happen because people believe. And I believe. (1994)

Having no reason to live is worse than death. We must give back to people the sense of fulfillment that comes from producing something they're proud of.

If you think and live in the future then you're out there chopping wood when most guys are planting trees.

XIX

Luck

The person who doesn't have it says, "He was just lucky."

◆━━━━━━━━━◆

You're lucky if you find something, but you have to be searching. It's like the prospector who goes out there for twenty years. Finally he finds something and everyone says, "That lucky S.O.B."

◆━━━━━━━━━◆

Winning an ice pool ticket is luck. That's why I don't gamble. That isn't real life.

ongshoreman philosopher Eric Hoffer said I was born with luck. I don't understand that. Luck comes disguised as work.

ne of my friends in high school used to say, "Wally is lucky not to get tackled. That's why he makes so many touchdowns." That wasn't luck. It was fear!

XX

Work

In America, the person of social conscience doesn't understand that it's not so much what you feed a man's belly, but what you feed his soul. They haven't understood why man works. They haven't grasped the spiritual side of work.

We'll soon get to the point where half of the population is not producing. They'll be in government. (1975)

President Lyndon Johnson was right to declare a war on poverty, but the public didn't understand that we had to go to work to win it.

It only becomes work when you don't enjoy doing it.

Work isn't work if you are having fun, and we're going to have fun.

(Inaugural Address—1990)

I inspect the boiler room. If it's clean, I don't worry about the guest rooms.

(As a hotel owner, Hickel often inspects other hotels, usually starting in the basement.)

When a man thinks he's too good to do another man's work, he neither understands work nor understands the man. I'm glad I was a bartender.

———◆———

If you think work is drudgery, try being unemployed.

———◆———

It takes just as much energy to pretend to mop the floor as to mop it. So mop it.

XXI

There's No Miracle to Success

There's no miracle to success.
You start from zero and you never quit.

Do something because people need it, and you will be wealthy. Do something just to make money, and you will eventually consider yourself a failure.

There's no retirement for the creative. It goes on forever.

If a man is a success, he's brilliant. If he's a failure, he's crazy. But he's still the same man.

If you build a one-room log cabin for your wife and child, you'll feel more secure than if you inherit a castle.

My success is in motivating people to do what I cannot.

The way to destroy an idea is to give it to someone who doesn't know how to make it happen.

❖―――――――❖

If you don't try to achieve success too quickly, you can maintain your freedom.

❖―――――――❖

No project I ever built made sense at the bottom line, and I made millions. I didn't study the bottom line. I studied the opportunity.

Right doesn't always win; if you don't know how to win.

———◆———

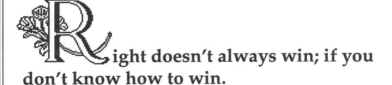o the maximum you can possibly do and one step more.

———◆———

Sometimes the road ahead isn't clear, but it's there. It clears up only as you walk it. (1973)

XXII

Taxes

Taxes are the reward for success. If you have no success, you pay no taxes.

❖━━━━━━━━━━━❖

I'd like to re-write the property tax laws of America. They penalize you for leaving open space. They force you to overbuild — to put towers on every lot.

❖━━━━━━━━━━━❖

They tax you into the beehive concept. They force you into ghettos. If it's a home, it should be taxed as a home. If it's a farm, it should be taxed as a farm. If it's a park, they should pay you to keep it in its natural state.

The U.S. government has to get off the attitude of deciding everything on a monetary basis. Neither the Friends of the Earth nor the banks can afford to pay the taxes to protect the open spaces we need.

———————————◆———————————

For every unemployable person you hire, government should let you deduct 120%. Sure beats welfare.

———————————◆———————————

Without production, there'll be no taxes. You don't get taxes from the poor.

XXIII

Free Enterprise

A successful businessman, Wally Hickel strongly believes in the free enterprise system. But he often talks about why it needs regulations and enlightened leadership.

Free enterprise left totally free will destroy itself.

◆━━━━━━━━◆

The most economical approach is to exploit the workers and ravage the environment. The whaling industry is a perfect example. The industry became so effective that all great whales faced extinction; and so did the industry.

◆━━━━━━━━◆

We've got freedom mixed up with business. Some proponents of free enterprise talk as if they were saying that Catholicism is the only true religion.

Private enterprise likes to blame government. They use it and then hide behind it.

We've exploited the developing nations under the guise of helping. They figured we'd be human, and we treated them as animals. We went under the white flag of truce, but we were pirates. I saw this first-hand in Alaska. I used to wonder if the canned salmon industry would do this to their own American citizens in Alaska, what would they do to Africa?

he primary purpose of business is to give: to give a return, to give service, to give employment, and to give to the unfortunate. Without any one of these, government must become involved.

hose in business must realize that the bottom line is important, but it is not the *only* line.

It sounds like a contradiction in terms, but the future demands "unselfish Capitalism."

Some labor leaders are asking for more pay for less work, but the answer is more pay for more work.

Some labor unions are making the mistake of making all the workers alike. Whether they are good workers or bad, they get paid the same, and get the same retirement. They are told not to show the other guy up, "Don't lay more bricks than the next guy." There is no incentive to create or produce.

In lieu of raises, unions should negotiate options for their people to acquire shares of stock. This would help them understand the obligations of ownership and management.

◆————————◆

You have to gain with gain, and lose with loss. That is the obligation of ownership. It's like marrying — for richer or poorer.

Management is getting lazy in America. The non-producers in Palm Springs, Palm Beach, or Palm Desert are waiting for the return on their stock, while the guys sweating on the assembly line are doing all the producing.

America will never go socialist. But we could go fascist under the guise of a free enterprise system.

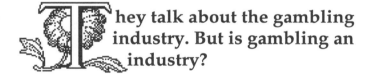The banks and the insurance companies have acquired too much power. What Teddy Roosevelt began at the turn of the century must now be completed.

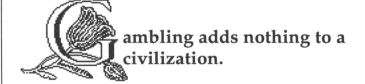They talk about the gambling industry. But is gambling an industry?

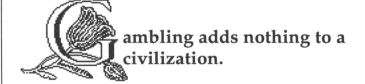Gambling adds nothing to a civilization.

XXIV

Peoples of the World

Wait till the happy face of Siberia overwhelms the sour face of Moscow. (1972)

It's going to be the slave who was shipped to Siberia who's going to make Russia great. (1974)

The Siberian is different from the European Russian. He's a warm human being and an optimist.

Siberia, the land of incentive. They are the incentive-minded people: not in a do-gooder sense but in a real sense.

◆————————————————◆

The Soviet Union could do big jobs well. They put men in space. But they couldn't get their potatoes across town.

If I were talking to the Russians, I would say, "Your strength is in your people not in your guns. I don't fear your guns, because I don't fear your people." (1975)

———◆———

Many Alaskans have Russian blood. Many of us have Russian names. Some of our Eskimo people and theirs speak the same language. Their traditions are our traditions. Their faith is our faith. All our saints are Russians. In short, we are a family of one.

———◆———

The Pacific is where the future is, because that's where the people are. That's where the needs are. That's where the opportunities are.

What I keep seeing more and more is not Washington, DC. It's what I saw as a boy . . . the Pacific. (1974)

The world isn't Europe or the moon. It's the Pacific, and it hasn't been discovered yet. (1973)

The balloon of Europe is full. Our opportunity is where people need help, and that is in the Pacific.

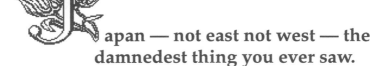 apan — not east not west — the damnedest thing you ever saw.

◆————————————◆

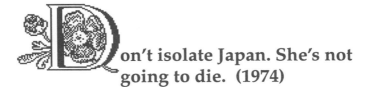he U.N. environmental program should be headquartered in Tokyo not Nairobi. (1972)

◆————————————◆

on't isolate Japan. She's not going to die. (1974)

Some of the Arab countries are like Russia before the revolution.

———◆———◆———

Latin America — the suppression is economic. Nations like Brazil may need a benevolent dictator, someone who is almost Christ-like but tougher than a boot.

———◆———◆———

China is of one mind. It will be one of the great production leaders of the 21st century. When you put that work force together with inexpensive energy, China will be unstoppable. (1979)

China is just going to wear you out.

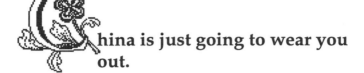

The poor are an opportunity. The rich are a problem. Think of the opportunity of a billion people in China.

I am sick and tired of those who say life is cheap in Asia. Life is only cheap when it is not your own.

XXV

Political Leadership

Who was more disciplined than Thomas Jefferson? Who was more free?

◆————————————————◆

The idle international cocktail set hated Harry Truman for being basic.

◆————————————————◆

The special interests finally wore Teddy Roosevelt down. He died of a broken heart. But his face is on Mt. Rushmore.

If Ralph Nader went into politics, he'd have to face all realities, not just his own. You can be in your own little world, and it can be anything from consumer protection to polar bears and be real, but it's not necessarily the total reality.

◆————————————◆

What has the Sierra Club ever done for the poor?

I'm not impressed with Henry Kissinger's diplomacy of intrigue. There's no intrigue in decency. The only time there's intrigue is for intrigue's sake, to make it look romantic. Win friends. That's diplomacy. I can't be wrong on this, because it's so basically right. (1974)

———◆———◆———

President Nixon's problem was the problem of the legal mind.

———◆———◆———

If President Nixon is innocent, I will stand up to 199 million Americans and defend him. If he's guilty, he must go. (May 7, 1973)

Richard Nixon says, "Pull yourself up by your bootstraps." Teddy Kennedy paints a picture of a new world, and the people expect everything to change overnight. Hickel says, "Let's build a building."(1973)

————◆————

Nixon was always amazed that it didn't bother me that he had fired me. There was no bitterness or resentment there. But, as I said at the time, "The president hired me, and he has the right to fire me." I put that behind me. I moved on, and we remained friends. (1994)

Governor Jay Hammond sees the way to protect the environment is to do nothing. I see the way to protect the environment is to clean up the mess.

◆————————————◆

John Kennedy had high-voltage enthusiasm. He ran his own show.

◆————————————◆

If Teddy Kennedy's name were Teddy Briscoe, he wouldn't be anything. He doesn't have the sense to come in out of the rain.

Ernest Gruening was one of the giants of Alaska history, not because of his size, but because of the size of the man inside the man. His principles were always bigger than he was. (1974)

To me, the greatest Alaskan was Judge James Wickersham. He brought about the Alaska Railroad, the first statehood bill, justice in remote areas, and the University of Alaska. As reward, he was probably the most persecuted politician in our history.

XXVI

Education
and
Creativity

It's as if we have deliberately culled out of the educational process all the real things of life.

———◆———

They're going to have schools in my lifetime where books are a sideline. (1973)

———◆———

America has confused education with intelligence.

Outside of the university classroom, economics is simple.

Tenure should be within a profession not within an institution.

Because what is absolute today is obsolete tomorrow, those who get their knowledge from books can't keep up. They operate from a basis of past knowledge.

Education should train the head, the hands and the heart.

———◆——————◆———

People get boxed in with too much education. If you just learn from books, not from your heart, you don't have that confidence.

———◆——————◆———

Vocational training is the top educational degree in the Arctic. It has nothing to do with status. It has to do with solving problems.

You learn more about decision–making on the football field than in the classroom.

When I got out of high school all I did was leave a building. It wasn't an achievement for me to get out. My education wasn't behind me, and I knew it.

Just because you have a college degree, and wear it like a sign around your neck, doesn't mean you're smart.

The weakness of predicting the future with a computer is that it can only compute on the basis of what is known. Computers have their place, but I have more faith in the creative capacity of man, and that's uncomputable

You can tell how well someone understands something by how simply he explains it.

XXVII

Law and Medicine

We need a generation of lawyers who will clean up the language of the law.

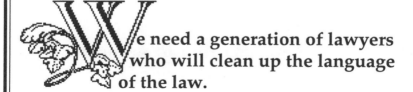

Law schools teach you how to turn your mind off from your conscience.

Morality is a higher level of legality. You can be legally right and completely morally wrong.

To separate your mind from your conscience for professional reasons to make a moral wrong legally right, doesn't make it right.

◆━━━━━━━━━━━◆

Doctors, supported by wild young attorneys showing them how to beat the system, are turning Medicare into a rip-off. (1975)

◆━━━━━━━━━━━◆

We need to take the mystery out of medicine.

Health is diet, exercise and attitude.

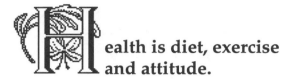

When asked why he gives his body such a thorough workout, often as much as an hour a day:

If you don't use it, it rusts.

It's not enough just to take care of the body and the mind. Health is the body, mind and soul.

XXVIII

The Highest and Best Use

We are in the midst of a civil war of priorities in this country, neighbor against neighbor, man against need, over preservation or use of nature and its resources. (1971)

There have been abuses of our natural resources. Yes. But there have been abuses to sex. You don't stop all sex. If man and production are the enemies, you would have to revert to the savage.

In the future, they will take food value from the fiber of a tree.

Everything on this earth has a reason. Not to be preserved for infinity, but to be used with reason.

❖————————————❖

Is it right to give a cow 100 acres of public land on which to roam, while we pen up a ghetto family in 100 square feet?

❖————————————❖

Fossil fuels will be used more and more for things of greater value than being burned in a boiler.

❖————————————❖

Eventually, Alaska will be shipping aspirin not oil.

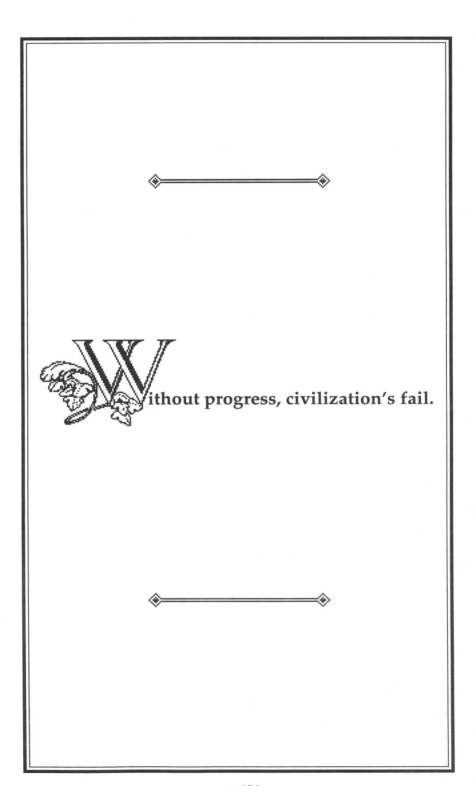

Without progress, civilization's fail.

XXIX

Family

Talk to your children when *they* want to listen.

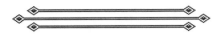

There's nothing happier than a happy family.

You mustn't over-protect a child. If he never has a chance to be exposed to realism, you will destroy him.

Being allowed the freedom to make mistakes is very important. My father allowed me to go into business at 18.

Don't put your children first, your wife first, or yourself first. Put first things first.

XXX

God and the "Little Guy"

I like to talk about God. Most politicians avoid it. Maybe they find him embarrassing. Maybe they think he's their competition.

God is the innovator. Man is the imitator.

For all its wonders, science hasn't discovered how to make an egg, add a little heat, and make a chicken.

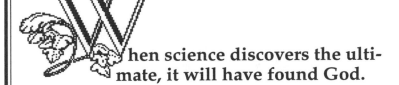

When science discovers the ultimate, it will have found God.

There are four billion people on earth, each with two eyes, a nose and a mouth, and all different. Technology could never do that. Only God could. God isn't dead; neither is hope. (1970)

It reached the ridiculous when a minority of a minority convinced the courts to expel God from the classroom.

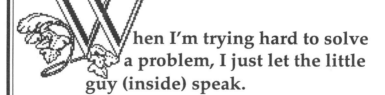

When I'm trying hard to solve a problem, I just let the little guy (inside) speak.

◆————————————◆

My little guy. He's my buddy. He never gets mad. Sometimes he hides. But then he comes out.

◆————————————◆

I get teased by the newspapers when I mention the little guy. But I don't care, because everyone has one. (1993)

God is in the mind.

I'm convinced that both heaven and hell are on earth. And the whole world is in one lifetime.

At a luncheon in Roveniemi, Finland, the Governor of Lapland asked Governor Hickel what he thought about his hometown Anchorage. He replied,

When I die, I hope to go there. (1994)

XXXI

Truth

A great mind makes truth simple. Moses did it.

◆————————————◆

I say only what I totally believe. You don't need to bug my phone. Just ask me.

◆————————————◆

Logic is not the whole truth, because it doesn't take into consideration the illogical.

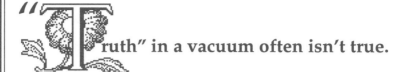

"Truth" in a vacuum often isn't true.

———◆———◆———

I don't want to read what a man says, or hear him say it. I want to *see* him say it.

———◆———◆———

You can tell a man's character in how he acts when it really gets tough in a political campaign.

ever take the child out of the human, and you'll always find the naked truth.

XXXII

Alaska First!

Excerpts from
the State of the State address
before the 18th Alaska State Legislature
Juneau, Alaska
January 11, 1994

r. President, Madam Speaker, members of the cabinet, fellow representatives of the people of Alaska, and Alaskans everywhere.

When we met here in this historic chamber three years ago, many for the first time, we spoke of a new beginning for Alaska. Well, we meet tonight to continue that work.

And if anyone expects a proud list of the accomplishments of this administration, I say let's leave that to the history books. And if anyone tells you that Alaska's best days are behind us, I say they're looking in the wrong direction. Let's roll up our sleeves. We have work to do.

Crime continues to spread fear in our cities. Families are failing. Health care and schools need reform. Seniors need better services. And rural Alaskans need jobs.

In addition, outside special interests continue to threaten Alaska's sovereign rights and our way of life. And oil prices are down — way down.

If anyone tells you that Alaska's best days are behind us, I say they're looking in the wrong direction.

Twenty-seven years ago, I stood in this chamber for the first time as Governor to address the State of the State. Jay Kerttula and Carl Moses were in the Chamber that day, then as now, as were U. S. Senator Ted Stevens, Anchorage Mayor Tom Fink, Congressman Don Young, and former State Senator Willie Hensley. And U.S. Senator Frank Murkowski was here, the youngest member of my cabinet.

That night in 1967 I set forth a simple, two-word phrase that has always been my guiding principle — Alaska First.

The challenge that night wasn't oil prices. We hadn't yet found the oil.

And yet, people were talking about crime. There was a considerable stir in the newspapers when it was revealed that a bunch of drivers' licenses had been issued in the names of Julius Caesar, Napoleon Bonaparte, and Abraham Lincoln.

Now, I know some of you think that I knew these great men personally. And, no doubt, we could use Lincoln's help to free Alaska from federal slavery. But that night I set forth a simple, two-word phrase that has always been my guiding principle — *Alaska First*.

I have worked hard every day of my adult life, as a builder and businessman, as Secretary of the Interior and as Governor, as a neighbor, a husband, a father and grandfather; on behalf of a single, lifelong mission — to do my damnedest for the country called Alaska.

Let's not let the price of oil blind us. We've got work to do.

Thursday night, when I speak to you on the State of the Budget, I will describe my plan for how to work our way through our revenue shortfall. I will outline our long-range options. And the course Alaska should take.

Unlike when oil prices dropped in 1986, we will not over-react. We have reserves to provide a bridge for the short-term. And for the mid-term and long-term, we have a multitude of options.

But tonight, let's not let the price of oil blind us. Tonight, we've got work to do.

Because putting *Alaska First* means confronting the epidemic of violence. Putting *Alaska First* means our schools must do better. Putting *Alaska First* means caring for our seniors. It means making health care accessible and affordable. And putting *Alaska First* means standing up to the federal government.

Education reform has momentum in Alaska. Our goal is simple — to graduate world-class students.

This is a full agenda. It's meant to be. And that means it's all out — right to the finish line.

Our kids deserve schools that are second to none. Not long ago I asked one student if he knew what the three "Rs" were. "Sure," he said, "Readin'. 'Ritin'. And *Remote control*."

"If I must choose between our kids' education and my reelection, I'm going with the *kids!*"

Education reform has momentum in Alaska. Our goal is simple — to graduate world-class students. World-class standards are being drafted for English, math, science and all major studies. And higher standards for the way colleges prepare our *teachers* will be ready by this spring.

Education reform may not be easy for those of you up for reelection. Those who protect the status quo may threaten to campaign against you. I don't know if *my* name will be on the ballot, but if it is, my answer will be this: "If I must choose between our kids' education and my reelection, I'm going with the *kids!*"

It's time we took another look at residency requirements in Alaska. Recently, the court ruled that anyone over 65, with just *one year* in the state, can qualify to enter our Pioneer Homes.

Over the past decade, a precedent has been set that destroyed the Longevity Bonus program. It makes our Permanent Fund Dividends a magnet for an invasion from Outside. And, if we don't do something, it will ruin our Pioneer Homes.

I've heard all the arguments. But I'm not convinced. Alaska is truly unique. The courts must understand this. We must try again. So I have asked the Department of Law to look once more at a preference system for Alaska's residents that can withstand constitutional challenge. Our pioneers have always put *Alaska First.* Let's do the same for them.

Someone said, "If it were possible to heal the family, it would be possible to heal the world." Let's ask the question, what can we do to strengthen Alaska's families?

First of all, we can fight alcohol and drug abuse. This is a crusade with many heroes, including Alaska's young people and someone very special to me. She has helped so many of our young people to say no to drugs and alcohol. First Lady Ermalee, much credit belongs to you, and I want to express to you, your husband's pride and Alaska's thanks. Surprised you didn't I?

We *all* need to look homeward. To look harder at how we nurture our families. To care for each other by "getting fit" — physically, emotionally, spiritually.

As we all know, one of the greatest stresses on families is health care. It costs too much. Yes, putting *Alaska First* means caring about both the cost and quality of Alaska's health care.

Always we are brought back to the issue of cost. We once again see the direct connection between economic development and com-passionate government. To be successful in our goals, we need revenue. And revenue comes from a healthy economy.

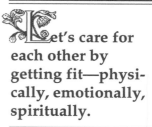

Let's care for each other by getting fit—physically, emotionally, spiritually.

And yet, outside groups are increasing their efforts to cram a "no growth, no progress" agenda down our throats. They seem to want an Alaska where no oil is drilled, no trees are harvested, no ore is taken from the ground nor fish from

Outside groups are increasing their efforts to cram a "no growth, no progress" agenda down our throats.

the sea, no fur is sewn, no ivory is carved by our Native craftsmen.

As a result, our young state is being treated as something less than we were promised; something less than an equal partner in this great American experiment of freedom; something less than a sovereign state endowed with an equal footing to all others.

Well, we Alaskans won't accept "something less."

It's time to let the word go out that no one dictates to us, and that we will not yield to outsiders what generations of Alaskans fought to create. It's time for Alaskans to take our country back.

Congress appears to have forgotten that the final road to statehood began not in Washington, DC but at the furthest reaches of the Alaska mail routes, in villages like Chilkat and Moose Pass.

It was August 26, 1958 — a brisk, clear, fall-like day. And outside 297 polling places, in schools and churches and post offices scattered across four time zones, Alaskans lined up to mark the first crude "X's" that grant the consent of the governed.

No bands marched. No fires were lighted, no bells rang out, no soldiers mustered. But sometime during the night, the awesome nature of Alaska changed for all time. For the first time in almost 50 years, another star was added to the Nation's flag.

On that day, nearly 50,000 Alaskans cast their ballots in the greatest free vote in the history of the territory. And with their votes, the people of Alaska literally signed a contract. They didn't just say "yes" to statehood. They agreed to the *terms* of statehood.

And that contract, like all contracts, cannot be changed without the consent of both parties. Congress made a deal not with Alaska's government — but with Alaska's *people*. It's time to honor that deal.

And that is why, over the past three years, together we have launched Alaska's *second battle for statehood.*

The story of Alaska is still being written by this administration and the men and women in this chamber. As Republicans, as Democrats, as Independents — we have closed ranks to truly put *Alaska First*. By launching a barrage of federal lawsuits, we have sent a shot across the bow of those in Washington, DC and across the nation who would pirate both Alaska's pocketbook and Alaska's purpose.

They choose to ignore that Alaska is showing other Arctic nations how to develop resources wisely. They choose to ignore that Alaska leads the nation in per capita spending on behalf of the environment and natural resources—$520 per person per year — according to the Council of State Governments. That's more than double the next state.

> **The people of Alaska literally signed a contract. They didn't just say "yes" to statehood. They agreed to the *terms* of statehood.**

By launching a barrage of federal lawsuits, we have sent a shot across the bow of those who would pirate both Alaska's pocketbook and Alaska's purpose.

They choose to ignore that while the federal government and most other states wrestle with how to define "sustainable development," Alaska is doing it.

The North Slope is home for the cleanest, most environmentally-responsible industrial project in the world. With additional exploration and the construction of a natural gas pipeline, we can see a "sustainable future" well into the next century. That's why we must stand up to Outside interests who would shut down our natural resource revenues.

This is not new in Alaska.

In 1967, I named a 34-year old attorney, the late George Boney, to the Alaska Supreme Court. He became Chief Justice. I said only one thing to George. "Don't let them steal the country."

He knew what I meant. I was referring to the mining interests at the turn of the century, and the canned salmon industry before statehood. There have always been absentee interests determined to control and exploit Alaska.

But to the next generation I say, let this be your rule: Let no special interest own you. Let no special interest divide you.

In the old days, it was never them and us. It was *all* of us. If we stay united we can solve our problems far better here than they can in Washington, DC.

I do not know if this will be my last opportunity to address you on the State of the State. Or whether this is the beginning of round two. But I know for sure that this year will be a defining year for Alaska.

As you debate Alaska's most important issues with each other, or as you and I — Mr. President and Madam Speaker — face off on difficult choices, let's keep one thing foremost in our hearts and minds.

We all love Alaska. Let's put *Alaska First!*

(Note: At this point the Governor handed ball caps to Senate President Rick Halford and House Speaker Ramona Barnes with "Alaska First!" embroidered on the front.)

And so tonight, a journey begins. We have work to do. Civilizations are what they think they are.

In much the same way that Carl Sandburg saw America, I see Alaska. I see Alaska not in the setting sun of a black night of despair. I see Alaska in the crimson light of a rising sun fresh from the burning, creative hand of God. I see great days ahead for men and women of will and vision.

 on't let them steal the country.

We can win the future and we can hand down to our children and grandchildren an Alaska even better than the one that was given to us.

I've never felt more strongly that Alaska's best days lie ahead.

And let us be sure that those who come after us will say of us, that we did everything that could be done. We finished the race. We kept Alaska strong. We kept the faith and put *Alaska First*.

God bless you, and God bless Alaska!

XXXIII

Famous Lines

I am not for conservation for conservation's sake. (1969)

❖————————————❖

Mike Wallace, on 60 Minutes, *asked Secretary Hickel if he planned to resign from President Nixon's cabinet. No, said Hickel, the President would have to fire him.*

If I leave, it will be with an arrow in my heart, not a bullet in my back. (1970)

As he placed the Blue Whale on the endangered species list, Secretary Hickel said,

It would be a crime beyond belief if in the same decade that man walked on the moon he destroyed the largest creature God ever put on earth. **(1970)**

Hickel sent one of the first copies of his best selling book Who Owns America? *to President Nixon with this inscription:*

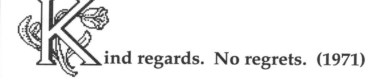

Kind regards. No regrets. **(1971)**

After being elected Governor of Alaska in 1966, Hickel was asked the perennial question: did he favor moving the capital from Juneau? His reply:

Let's quit talking about moving the capital. Let's get the capital moving. **(1966)**

The winning argument in a debate with several cabinet officers as they discussed the Alaska Native land claims with President Nixon:

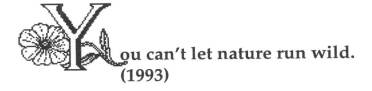**W**hether or not they have a legal claim, they have a moral claim. **(1969)**

Explaining why the Alaska Department of Fish and Game must reduce the number of wolves to protect moose and caribou populations:

You can't let nature run wild. **(1993)**

From his celebrated letter to President Nixon after the killings at Kent State University by the Ohio National Guard:

If we read history, it clearly shows that youth in its protest must be heard. (1970)

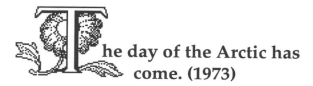

Title of article in the Reader's Digest:

The day of the Arctic has come. (1973)

XXXIV

Big Projects

In the Arctic, it takes big projects. If the Prudhoe Bay oil reservoir had only one billion barrels in it, they never would have built the trans-Alaska pipeline.

———◆———◆———

Anything that is conceivable in the human mind is possible.

The oil industry and the conservationists fought my idea of a railroad to the North Slope. Later they both apologized. We could have thrown away that railroad after the trans-Alaska pipeline was built for the money it would have saved.

———————◆———————

The most necessary resource of the next century will be fresh water.

———————◆———————

Let's lay a large diameter pipe on the ocean floor to carry fresh water from Alaska to the South 48. (1978)

For a dollar a day a person, I'll give Californians all the water they want. (1991)

With the right approach, downtown Tokyo could become a park.

Without World War II, we may have never had the courage to build the Alaska Highway. But we built it in nine months — the length of a pregnancy.

We need that sense of expectation that says, "Let's put a man in the galaxies."

◆━━━━━━━━━━━━◆

To say there is no money for a big project is an excuse. On December 6, 1941, we had no money. The next day we mobilized the nation.

◆━━━━━━━━━━━━◆

If God didn't like big projects, he wouldn't have created the universe.

XXXV

Why war?
Why not big projects?

Excerpts from an
address to the 47th annual
U.N. Department of Public Information/
Non-Governmental Organization Conference,
"We the Peoples: Building Peace"
United Nations Headquarters,
New York, New York,
September 22, 1994.

Today I bring to you a proposal for the next century. I commend it to all nations for their best thinking and creativity.

Philosophers have talked for centuries about building a new world. Today we are meeting to discuss building peace. My conclusion is that to build a new world — to build peace — we must literally build it.

Historically, the world's most cynical leaders have used war or preparing for war as an economic strategy. War puts people to work and gives them a purpose. War concentrates the thoughts of a nation, making it think and act as one.

Why war? Why not big projects? After all, war is just a big project.

But why war? Why not big projects? After all, war is just a big project.

The price of freedom doesn't have to be blood. It can be sweat.

My idea is not new. It's as old as the pyramids and the aqueducts of Rome.

In our own time, Masaki Nakajima has led the way with his Global Infrastructure Fund.

And the late inventor Buckminister Fuller conceived of a global energy network, linking the industrial and developing worlds with an energy grid. Existing electrical generators, unused during the night in the North, can be tapped — at the speed of light — to bring poverty-fighting power to the South.

Two billion people live without electricity today. Show me any area in the world where there is a lack of energy, and I'll show you basic poverty. There is a direct tie-in between energy and poverty, energy and war, energy and peace.

While Fuller's global concept may seem like science fiction, electrical interconnections between regions — and even continents — can and must be tackled now. This can be a vast and visionary undertaking — worthy of our generation.

Some people may ask, "Where will the money come from?" I say money is not the problem. There's always enough money to go to war. It all depends on our priorities.

There's always enough money to go to war

In some quarters, big projects today are not "politically correct." But if God didn't like big projects, He wouldn't have created the universe.

Many sincere people believe "small is beautiful" and "wilderness is the world." But we in the Far North understand the power of a big project to change society. Russia did it with the 6,500 mile trans-Siberia Railway. Alaska did it when we built the largest project in the history of free enterprise, the trans-Alaska oil pipeline. It mobilized our people, gave them a challenge, and a goal.

We in the Far North understand the power of a big project to change society.

I have talked about longline energy grids with my fellow governors in The Northern Forum, an organization of 24 Arctic regions. And we have discussed sharing our vast fresh water resources in the North with the arid nations of the South. We are planning to use our vast natural gas resources to help clean up the smog-choked cities of the industrial world.

And we have dreamed about a rail tunnel beneath the Bering Sea. Imagine, a rail trip from New York through Alaska, connecting with the trans-Siberia railway, and on to Paris, circling more than halfway around the world, and carrying with it a wealth of ideas, of commerce, and of wonder.

For water transport, the regions of The Northern Forum are already working to make Russia's Northern Sea Route a common carrier for the world's goods. For example, resources from the Pacific Northwest of the United States of America — transported on ice-armored freighters over the top of the world — can arrive in Rotterdam eight days faster than if they sail through the Panama Canal. Japanese cargo can get there a remarkable 18 days faster.

The solution to our social problems is not money. It is productive work. And the best jobs are those with a sense of mission. The builders of the great monuments of the world proved that centuries ago — the craftsmen who constructed the cathedrals of Europe; the Africans who designed and built the pyramids; the Mayans who created ancient temples in America; the Khmer who built Angkor Wat. For some, putting those stones in place was a religious experience of its own.

Today, where do the tourists of the world want to go? They visit those shrines. They want to see the Statue of Liberty and Washington, DC, with its marvelous monuments and architecture, the Eiffel Tower, the Taj Mahal, St. Petersburg, the Sistine Chapel, the Parthenon.

> The solution to our social problems is not money. It is productive work. And the best jobs are those with a sense of mission.

And it is not just monuments that attract. Great engineering achievements do, too — the Great Wall of China, the Suez Canal, Machu Picchu in Peru, and the Sydney

Opera House. And even in Alaska many of our visitors want to see and touch the 789-mile trans-Alaska pipeline.

Mankind's handiwork fascinates and inspires every generation.

As we approach the end of this century, let's agree on some big projects and build them.

So, as we approach the end of this century, let's agree on some big projects and build them. Let's link up the world's excess electrical generating capacity with those most in need. Let's take water from North to South. Let's construct the Bering Tunnel and join the world's continents. Let's harvest the wealth of northern resources, especially our storehouse of energy.

If we tackle these projects, we will learn that the days of pioneering are not over.

XXXVI

Humor

I think "bullshit" said at the right time communicates the total.

❖━━━━━━━❖

Referring to the Copper River Scenic Highway:

Some mistakes were made. That's the problem when you have a Department of Transportation that hasn't built a road in fifteen years. When you finally say "Go," the enthusiasm is overwhelming! (State of the State, 1992)

Nixon misreads me. So does the nation. Just because I crawled out of a snake pit doesn't mean I'm a snake. (1973)

❖————————❖

If I owned a newspaper, one day I would run a banner headline that read, "NO NEWS TODAY."

Explaining to the legislature why the Alaska Longevity Bonus program had to be phased out:

f those who fit the original criteria, only a few are alive today. And I should know. The very first list had just three names on it. Vitus Bering. Lord Baranof. And me. **(1993)**

In 1970, Senator Joseph Montoya of New Mexico wrote an angry, unanswerable letter to Interior Secretary Hickel. After being pressed for several days by his assistant Dave Parker to dictate a response, Hickel exploded, "Take down this telegram.

uck you. Strong letter follows."

In the legislature during an election year, there are no friends and no enemies. They are *all* opposition.

◆————————◆

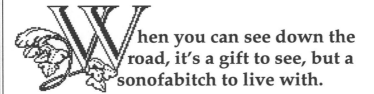

When you can see down the road, it's a gift to see, but a sonofabitch to live with.

I don't want to be President. Of course, it would be an honor. They'd probably build a library in my memory and put a lot of comic books in it!

I'll keep fighting for what I believe in forever. That's why I told my wife, Ermalee, to bury me standing up.

XXXVII

Four Thoughts for the World

Someone has to recognize that all the people on the earth are human.

We need a total world monetary system.

Those things that are owned by no one are owned by the total.

Dream big dreams. Because if you dream little dreams, you can only achieve little things. But if you dream big dreams, you can achieve little things and big things.

ACKNOWLEDGEMENTS

Yvonne Esbensen Lindblom typed and retyped these thoughts and sayings and kept many of them in safe-keeping for years. She even cleaned up a few. Darrell Chambers, after serving as a Hartig Fellow at Commonwealth North, used his wizardry with a computer to create this book's happy lay-out. Years later he re-designed the book, page by page. Matt Knutson designed the cover and made final adjustments on the layout. Tom Hughes provided advice and encouragement. My outstanding secretary, Patti Gilbert, combed every quote for typos and grammatical errors. John Hendrickson of the Governor's staff suggested several of the more recent lines. Ed McNally, Alaska's District Attorney and a gifted writer, added inspiration. And my wife, Cindy and our three kids, cheered me on in the often lonely work of late-night design and editing.

Mead Treadwell, another longtime Hickel aide and colleague, first suggested the idea of this book as a gift for Hickel's seventieth birthday. One day, Mead will surely compile his own volume of "Hickelisms."

To all these individuals, I owe my heartfelt thanks. Most of all my gratitude goes to the originator of these ideas who gets such pleasure from framing thoughts in ways that will be remembered.

— M. B. Roberts

Photo by Yvonne Lindblom

R aised on a small citrus ranch in Southern California, Malcolm B. Roberts joined Walter J. Hickel's staff at the U.S. Department of the Interior in 1970 (see photo above, taken in Rock Creek Park during one of Secretary Hickel's frequent horseback rides). Off and on since then, Roberts has worked with Hickel, as the first Executive Director of Commonwealth North, a public policy forum created by Hickel and the late Governor William A. Egan in Anchorage, Alaska, and as a Special Assistant in Juneau during Hickel's second term as Governor.

Roberts graduated from Princeton University and soon afterwards helped form *Up with People*, an educational and musical experience for young people. For five years, he wrote an opinion column for the *Anchorage Daily News* and in 1990 edited the Commonwealth North study entitled *Going Up in Flames: the Promises and Pledges of Alaska Statehood Under Attack*. In addition to his work with Hickel, he claims as his greatest achievements his marriage to Cindy Graham Roberts of Auburn, California, who won the title of Mrs. America in 1978, and his part in raising their three talented children.